W9-CLK-607

flower
arranging
made
simple

40 FABULOUS IDEAS TO MAKE AT HOME

flower arranging made simple

40 FABULOUS IDEAS TO MAKE AT HOME

Jamie Aston

Photography by Ditte Isager

SASKATOON PUBLIC LIBRARY

Kyle Cathie Limited

For Lynn, John and Lisa

First published in Great Britain in 2007 by
Kyle Cathie Limited
122 Arlington Road
London NW1 7HP
general.enquiries@kyle-cathie.com
www.kylecathie.com

10 9 8 7 6 5 4 3 2 1

ISBN 978 1 85626 717 5

Text © 2007 Jamie Aston
Photography © 2007 Ditte Isager
Book design © 2007 Kyle Cathie Limited

All rights reserved. No reproduction, copy or transmission of
this publication may be made without written permission. No
paragraph of this publication may be reproduced, copied or
transmitted save with the written permission or in accordance
with the provision of the Copyright Act 1956 (as amended).
Any person who does any unauthorised act in relation to this
publication may be liable to criminal prosecution and civil
claims for damages.

Project editor Jennifer Wheatley
Designer and Art Director Nicky Collings
Photographer Ditte Isager
Styling Tabitha Hawkins
Copy editor Vanessa Kendell
Editorial assistant Vicki Murrell
Production Sha Huxtable and Alice Holloway

Jamie Aston is hereby identified as the author of this work
in accordance with Section 77 of the Copyright, Designs and
Patents Act 1988.

A Cataloguing In Publication record for this title is available
from the British Library.

Printed in China

contents

introduction

Flower arranging has always been something I've had a passion for. Like most flower enthusiasts, I started out buying flowers from my local florists and trying out ways of displaying them at home. Of course, these experiments did not always work exactly as I thought they would. When I look at some of the photographs I proudly shot some years back, it's easy to see my designs were a little hit and miss! However, my floristry improved in leaps and bounds once I started looking at the different flowers available and researching the work of leading florists. I can remember the first time I saw a salmon-coloured amaryllis, thinking it was the most beautiful flower I had ever seen. I bought a few stems and arranged them into a bouquet for my mother – little did I know that I had picked one of the hardest flower stems to hand tie. I can also remember arranging 25 red roses with willow from the garden for my parents' anniversary. It ended up being a little on the big side and slightly over the top. Over the years, I have learned to keep my designs simple and elegant and not overdo things.

When I decided that I wanted to pursue floristry as a full-time career, I wanted to learn all I could as quickly as I could. I decided to volunteer at a local flower shop, and this I found is the best way of learning. You can't beat actually experiencing everything first-hand. I volunteered full time for a number of months, then I headed for London. I enrolled on a career course in floristry, much like the courses we now run at our school. This short intensive course taught me all the basic principles behind modern-day floristry which then gave me the confidence to start breaking the rules.

Flower arranging really isn't that hard. We can all do the very basics, such as choose flowers that are appropriate for an occasion, but it suddenly becomes daunting when it comes to arranging flowers in a vase or on a table. I hope this book guides you well, and gives you the inspiration and confidence to start enjoying arranging with flowers.

my flower school

Flower arranging has never been so hip. The industry is full of talented people all pushing the boundaries of modern-day floristry. One part of the industry, however, that has failed to change is the training process. Options for students are limited to poor training courses with uninspiring curriculums.

One part of my job I enjoy the most is teaching students in our flower school. Our students are from all over the world. They come to our school for one-day workshops just to have some fun and learn new skills. They can never quite believe what they have made at the end of the day. This is the part I love: proving to people their capabilities.

So many students who come to me have little or no confidence in their work. It's a common occurrence; old-fashioned methods are drilled into students who, in turn, become nervous wrecks at the thought of having to make a bouquet or even create a simple vase display. One class I taught in Japan found it incredibly difficult to arrange flowers in a vase where the flowers were more than two-thirds the height of the vase, yet another old-fashioned rule worth breaking!

Why does it have to be so hard? Flower arranging should be enjoyable. You only need a little guidance to get yourself started. Once you start learning what works for you and which flowers go together, your confidence will improve. I believe confidence in what you do – even if what you're making is not quite working – is the key. You need to develop the confidence to try new looks, use different flowers and mix contrasting colours, and find your own style. You'll only do this by making mistakes!

Over the years, I have learned the most from my mistakes, not from my successes. You need to give your mistakes in floristry a positive angle. I remember when I first had to make a large pedestal with floral foam. My boss looked on as I started to arrange my flowers into the wrong-sized blocks of foam. I didn't know back then that the foam size I had chosen was not going to hold all the flowers I needed to arrange. Needless to say, I made my display and as I went to move it the whole thing fell apart! Only then did my boss decide to tell me what I should have done. Despite being angry at the time, I never repeated my mistake. You will find that as you try to make any of the designs in this book, you are bound to make mistakes, but the key is to shrug them off and keep going.

I'm sure I sound like some know-it-all; I don't know it all, but I do know what works and how to instil confidence into students to make something they never thought possible. I believe it can be very simple to get real results with just a little guidance. I try to make it a relaxed process. There are no rules, just guidelines. This book, I hope, will show you that. As you flick through the pages and try out a few of the projects, you will learn just how easy it can be to create simple, effective floral displays.

USING THIS BOOK

This book contains 40 easy-to-follow ideas that are ideal for making at home, either on your own or with your friends or children. I have tried to keep all the designs as simple as I can and every project has clear and informative step-by-step instructions and pictures for you to follow.

Each project demonstrates a particular technique. For example, making the buttonholes will teach you about wiring, and you'll learn how to spiral stems in making the hand-tied bouquet. I've suggested variations in each case, so you can play with different flowers and colours according to your own personal taste.

The intention of this book is to show you just how effortless it can be to create professional standards of work with ease. There are no immensely difficult projects in this book, just unfussy, practical designs that you can easily create yourself at home.

choosing flowers

Flower shops are the best places to buy your flowers. The staff can advise and assist you with any queries you have. Flower shops also generally have a wide stock of flowers and a great atmosphere. You can't beat the smell and vibe you get in a real flower shop. Supermarkets, garden centres and flower markets will offer you a good selection and superior freshness in many cases, but remember the freshest-looking flowers do not always indicate the best quality.

When it comes to buying your flowers from your local florist, garden centre or supermarket, you need to bear a few things in mind. You are looking for the best your money can buy – this will often mean the flowers with the most life left in them with the biggest heads or buds, the strongest stems, the stems with the most heads and the sweetest of scents.

Your flower shop will have a selection of flowers at different stages. You might find a daily specials area with flowers going cheap – great for parties where they only need to last for the evening or a couple of days.

Flower shops are also able to stock unusual varieties of flowers. At Jamie Aston, we are constantly receiving deliveries from Italy of some of the biggest and more unusual flowers available. For example, this year we were awash with six-feet-high dahlias in a multitude of colours and blooms the size of a human head. This is only ever going to be available in a real flower shop.

To guarantee you get what you want, order your flowers from your florist in advance. Most flower shops will ask for a week's notice at the most for a specific order. Agree a price with your florist – this will avoid any surprises when you collect your flowers!

Ethical flowers

You might want to check with your florist, and indeed your supermarket, if your flowers are fair trade. Flowers are now hitting the market at very competitive prices, but they are often grown in countries where production staff work 18-hour days with pesticides and inhumane working conditions. If you can afford to purchase flowers, on all accounts a luxury item, then you should not be purchasing them from such channels of distribution. It's also a good idea to check where your flowers have come from if you are concerned with your carbon footprint. For example, you can now buy peonies in spring from New Zealand at a much lower price compared with those bought in season from Holland.

A few things to look out for:

Look at the foliage below the flowers. This can often indicate how old the flower is if, for example, the leaves are wilting and/or mouldy.

Check for signs of mould or infection; flowers such as celosia can often be found with a black mould growing in between the grooves of the flower. This will spread and end up killing the flowers before you have had the chance to enjoy them.

Roses You can check if a rose is fresh by looking at it, but also by gently squeezing the bottom of the head. If the rose feels tight and hard, this normally indicates it's very fresh. When it feels loose and soft, it's not so fresh.

Peonies often come in with little ball-shaped buds as hard as bullets. Sometimes these buds disappoint and fail to open. Don't buy peonies with sticky buds, because these have been picked too early and will probably not open.

Hydrangea, lilac, viburnum and other woody-stemmed flowers Always ensure your florist provides you with the correct flower food specially designed for woody stems.

colour

Flowers never fail to amaze me. With growers producing them in so many vibrant shades each year, there is never a dull moment. When I first started in floristry, I was slightly scared of colour – I was too conscious of overdoing it and creating something garish. It can be very difficult to gain the confidence to start mixing colours together when you first start out. There are, however, a few easy guidelines when it comes to working with colour.

Colour wheel

The photograph on the right shows my interpretation of a colour wheel, made from rose heads. Colour wheels come in various levels of complexity, but the basic idea is that they represent the colours of the rainbow going round in a circle. The theory is that any colours that lie next to each other on the wheel go well together – these are known as 'toning' colours. Colours that are opposite each other on the colour wheel – 'complementary' colours – are also supposed to go together, because they contrast with one another: these pairs are orange and blue, red and green, and purple and yellow.

Toning colours

By toning colours, I mean different shades of the same basic colour. It's a safe bet to pick two colours that lie next to each other on the colour wheel and use flowers in different shades of them for an arrangement, such as lilac and blue, or purple and pink. To visualise different shades of a colour, imagine taking one colour, red for example, and watering it down. The more water you add the lighter the colour will become.

Complementary colours

This is where I like to break the rules, because I do not believe that complementary colours always work well together. What looks good on paper does not always look good in real life, but as ever it comes down to personal preference and taste. I personally would never wear a yellow jumper twinned with purple trousers, nor would I furnish my home with lime green and salmon curtains, so why would I want to put these colours together in a flower arrangement? Arrangements in clashing colours can either look fabulous or hideous. To pull it off, you need to stick to just a few colours and flowers. Until you become more confident, I would recommend sticking to toning colours.

Using white

In general, I avoid mixing white flowers with other colours, because they tend to dominate an arrangement, and make it look cheap and somewhat dated. However, white and green is one combination that always looks elegant. White and green bouquets are probably the best selling ones in my shop – they are neutral and classy and therefore complement any interior. White and green arrangements can look classic or contemporary depending on the flowers you use – putting some architectural-looking foliage or green tropical flowers, such as anthuriums or cymbidium orchids, in the mix will bring it right up to date. White and pale blue can sometimes work as well – reminiscent of Delft pottery. Again, this combination gives quite a classic look (see the hallway display on page 38). White and red is bad luck in floristry, because it is associated with blood and bandages!

Massing colours

A large mass of different colours becomes confusing for the eye, making it hard to focus on any particular part of the display. I always suggest to students that they aim to stick to one colour when trying to create something with real impact. Whenever I need to create something for an event or wedding that really stands out, I often mass one flower type of the same colour together in a huge display. A great big urn of tulips all of the same colour has huge impact – even though the flower is quite ordinary, the effect of massing lots of them together never fails to make a statement and provide a focal point. You can achieve the same effect on a smaller scale by choosing one or two flowers of different textures and grouping them in vases of different heights. Here I have used fiery orange roses and nutans and grouped them in dark smoky vases for a really dramatic display.

To the right are lists of various colour combinations: some tried-and-tested ones that always work and some that I think should be avoided. The colours I have listed as working well together are just my opinion, and this is founded on what's going on around me, such as trends in interiors, as well as my personal preference.

Once you feel happy working with my colour combinations, you'll have the confidence to experiment with your own ideas. It's important to trust your instincts and think carefully about where you are going to be placing your flowers or what you will be using them for. If your theme is multicoloured and the room the flowers are going in is of that nature, then why not just go for it with the flowers? Sometimes guidelines can be stretched, too.

See, it's easy. You really don't have to try too hard, just follow the basic guidelines and you can't go wrong.

a few tried-and-trusted colour combinations

- Bright orange and hot pink
- Red and hot pink
- Green and white
- Purple and pink
- Burnt orange and yellow
- Lilac and blue

bad colour combinations

- Purple and yellow
- Red and white
- Bright orange and green
- Orange and blue
- Lime green and salmon
- Multicoloured! Never a good look

style

It's not only important to get the colours right, but also the style of your display. It's like saying location, location, location. Style, style, style is the key to a successful display. This section is all about styling, mixing textures together and getting the most from your selection of flowers. There are so many different looks out there it would be wrong to just pick one style and say that's all I'm going to make from now on. So be bold and have a go at these four basic styles: country garden, woodland, architectural and tropical.

COUNTRY GARDEN

This typically English style reflects all that is summery and fresh. A country-garden display always reminds me of home. The flowers are always bloomy and full of bright colours and fluffy textures, and the foliage often includes garden herbs. This style of arrangement seems to be universally popular because I think people see it as relaxed and informal, almost non-threatening. It's not the sort of style that you find in offices or corporate buildings, but it's all the rage right now, with all that's old-fashioned and floral becoming popular again. Country garden has to be one of the easiest of styles to achieve. Just placing some flowers into an old water jug, or massing garden flowers together in any container you can find will do the job.

• Flowers that are best suited to this style are dahlias, roses, peonies, hydrangeas, delphiniums and viburnum. I like to use garden herbs instead of foliage; mint, lavender, sage and rosemary are ideal.

• Vases and containers should be rustic, old tin pots, milk jugs – even vintage crystal vases all work well.

• My favourite way of using this style is to mass a large selection of different-sized bottles on a table and fill each one with a stem or two of the flowers I've listed. Mixing mint and lavender through them adds scent.

• Country garden can be mixed successfully with other rustic styles such as Woodland, but does not go so well with more contemporary styles, such as Tropical and Architectural.

WOODLAND

Rugged textures, berries, bark and moss all fall under this category. It's not a style you see that often when it comes to flower arranging, but I quite like it.

It has an almost autumnal feel, as the flowers are often burnt oranges and dirty greens and browns. I guess it's not the prettiest of styles, but in a contemporary home with white-washed walls, it comes into its own. I remember Christmases at home when I used to trot off down to the woods and gather cones and branches of pine, bring them home and use them to decorate the stairway or make them into a huge garland for the fireplace. It's very satisfying to make something gorgeous from materials you have sourced for free!

• Bark, husks, berries, cones, twigs, lichens and moss can all be found in the woods, or sourced from your local florist. Hypericum, crab apples and rosehips also fit in this category. Flowers such as bluebells, snowdrops and strawberry flowers picked from your garden all add to a convincing woodland style.

• The beauty about this style is that you don't need to spend a fortune at your local florist on any of the products. Take a trip down to the woods and everything you need will be around you.

• I would suggest placing some bark or husk into a tall clear vase on its own. This would be a very unusual arrangement, and very striking in the modern home.

• Woodland makes a very good base for other styles, such as Country Garden – just make sure the colours complement each other.

ARCHITECTURAL

Visually striking, clean and simple, architectural displays work well in minimal environments. These can come across rather cold, but their impact can be incredibly strong. I quite like this style, particularly in my home. I like the simplicity of a vase filled with interesting leaves or grasses. I also like to shock people when they come to my home – everyone always expects a house full of flowers, but when they see grasses and leaves massed in clear glass vases, they're surprised at how well it actually works. This kind of display makes you think about nature and what's on display. An elegant vase full of the most boring leaves suddenly becomes interesting.

• Alocasia leaves, kentia leaves and palm leaves, snake grass, china grass, steel grass and lily grass all work well in architectural displays. Bamboo and sugar cane can also be easily sourced and work well. For flowers I would suggest anthuriums, gingers and proteas.

• I love tall shoots of steel grass en masse or a great big bunch of sugar cane encased inside a tall clear vase. These displays can come across masculine with their clean elegance.

• Architectural displays work best when arranged in tall clear glass vases, or simple white- or black-coloured glass vases.

• The added advantage with these kinds of displays is their longevity; they can last for weeks – you just need to keep changing the water.

• Architectural displays work well when twinned with Woodland and Tropical arrangements. In my opinion, they do not work so well when mixed with a Country Garden display.

TROPICAL

I have to say this is probably my least favourite of the four styles. Tropical flowers can be incredibly bright and somewhat plastic in appearance. I think my dislike for these flowers comes from seeing them in every mundane restaurant and office building across the country. They are used heavily in corporate work by florists, because they last so well and give maximum impact. Used well, however, tropical displays can be a lot of fun and are best suited to relaxed informal events, such as Hawaiian-themed parties.

• The most common tropical flowers are orchids, anthuriums, heliconias, strelitzias, gingers and cordyline leaves. Orchids are my preferred tropical flower. They come in so many diverse varieties. The most popular readily available orchids are cymbidium and phalaenopsis orchids.

• I like to fill tall clear glass spaghetti vases with large cymbidium orchids. This simple design, as featured in this book (see page 42), works incredibly well. It has a real contemporary feel.

• If you're feeling bright and cheery and want to make a statement, I recommend massing a bundle of hot pink gingers and variegated pink cordyline leaves together in a clear vase full of vivid pink water! A couple of drops of food colouring does the trick.

• Most tropical flowers keep incredibly well, with some orchid varieties lasting three to four weeks. Anthuriums and heliconias also last for weeks when looked after and cared for properly.

flower shopping lists

These days it is almost possible to get any flower you want at any time of the year for a price, but quality is not always guaranteed out of season. I have outlined a few flower 'shopping lists' below, which show you what's around each season – this means flowers at a good price and at their very best. For each season, I've suggested some combinations of flowers that will work well as a group, whether you choose to put them in a vase, an arrangement or a bouquet.

SPRING

Probably my favourite time of year with regards to flowers. It's always inspiring on the early spring mornings at the flower market when you start to see all the bright spring flowers coming into season. Spring flowers are often competitively priced and highly scented which makes them even more attractive.

For an arrangement that screams springtime

Double French pink tulips

Pale pink helleborus

Pink hyacinths

Lime green viburnum

Pale pink cherry blossom

Fragrant hints of yellow

Forsythia

Green antirrhinum

White tuberose

Paper whites

Pretty and delicate

Pale blue muscari

Lilac camellia

Blue nigella

Lilac

Lilac iris

SUMMER

This is always a hard time for florists; flowers never seem to last all that well with the heat, but you can't beat a large fresh display in the house. It's almost like bringing the garden inside.

Blousy summer

Hot pink peonies

Orange dahlias

Hot pink sweet peas

Lime green viburnum

Pink ranunculus

From the garden

White delphiniums

White hydrangeas

White agapanthus

White stocks

White lilac

Lily of the valley

White lupins

Quirky

Orange celosia

Yellow protea

Orange nutans

Sunflowers

Green amaranthus

Campanula

AUTUMN

Flower choices start to become a little limited through autumn and winter. However, you can still make the most of the season with the following lists. I personally love gladioli; they are at their best this time of year and lend themselves to tall vase displays that can never fail to cheer you up on an autumn day.

My favourites
Pale pink chrysanthemums
Pink or green sedum
White or pink snowberries
Pale pink gladioli

Unusual mix
Red euphorbia
Orange celosia
Orange calla lilies
Red gerbera

Understated mix
Green hypericum
Pink roses
Pink dahlias
Pale pink bouvardias

WINTER

Probably the most challenging time of year when it comes to flower availability and selection. This is when I always make good use of amaryllis, poinsettia and ilex berries. These flowers last for weeks and create a bold statement when used on their own. Try to incorporate any garden foliage you can find, such as pine, birch branches and holly, through your displays to help fill them out and add texture.

Best on their own in any colour

Amaryllis

Ilex berries

Poinsettia

Cotton

Rustic winter

Arum lilies

Brown anthuriums

Pink vintage roses

Moss- and lichen-covered twigs

Tropical

Red gingers

Dark brown anthuriums

Orangey red capsicums

Bottlebrushes

Yellow or orange nutans

23

choosing vases

Choosing the right vase can make even the most ordinary of flowers look stunning. In my opinion, vases are as important as the flowers when it comes to creating a beautiful display for the home – they really can help lift and add excitement. So with vases playing a major part in flower arranging, why do we all seem to have a stock of useless and hard-to-use ones in our homes?

BEST VASES

Here are my top four vases. If you are strapped for cash, invest in a simple glass cube vase and/or a clear glass fishbowl vase, both of which are readily available.

Bottle vase

Bottle vases are quirky and easy to use. Simply place a few stems of whatever fits into the vase. These vases work best in groups of two or three. I prefer to mass lots of different-sized bottle vases together, each holding a single flower stem.

Fishbowl vase

These offer you huge scope for arranging flowers. You can swirl soft-stemmed flowers around the inside, float flower heads and candles in them, or just use them as you would a regular vase. Large vases work well on kitchen or hallway tables filled with tulips curled inside (see page 36), along with some coloured gravel in the bottom.

Cube vase

Whether clear glass or coloured, cube vases are immensely useful, and ideal for housing the modern-day, hand-tied bouquet. They also come in handy for smaller bunches of flowers from your garden, or for floating single flower heads inside.

Spaghetti vases

The spaghetti vase is just a simple glass column vase that comes in many different heights (see page 27). These vases give you an impressive display with minimal effort and are great for lining up different flowers – a good look for a contemporary dinner party (see page 88). The only downside is reaching into these vases to clean them! Use a sponge on a stick.

WORST VASES

I'm sure we all have vases that become wider towards the top, as well as vases that are bulbous with very wide tops. These are incredibly difficult to use unless you have a mass of flowers. They also do not take kindly to hand-tied bouquets with their short stems and compact nature – they just look silly sitting in tall vases that swallow them up. Even the most experienced of florists spend time reorganising arrangements in hard-to-use vases. I have singled out three vases that I find difficult to use. I call these vases (pictured from left to right) the traditional vase, the open-neck vase and the V-shaped vase.

Traditional vase

This is actually not so difficult to use; its bulbous shape lends itself to tall, long-stemmed flowers and a loose display. However, whatever you do with this vase you will never get away from its dated look. It's almost as if the vase is working against the flowers. If you have one of these vases, I suggest filling it very loosely with old-fashioned, country-style flowers.

Open-neck vase

Now this vase is difficult to use. You will more than likely find yourself wanting to throw the vase on the floor in anger and frustration. Because of its narrow bottom and very wide neck, all the flowers are forced together and fail to fill the whole neck of the vase. This vase is best suited to modern architectural displays with subtle bendy flower stems that will fill the whole neck with ease, such as tulips.

V-shaped vase

This is one of the more common vases you might see in the modern flower shop. They are great when you

have a mass of flowers, say 60 roses to fill it with, but if you are not a flower shop and your budget doesn't allow you to go out and buy that many roses, this vase can be a bit greedy. Because it gets wider and wider towards the neck, flowers just sink down inside. You need tall stems and plenty of them for this vase. I remember having to use these vases when I was training for weekly office contracts. It was such a struggle filling them with what little we had in the way of flowers for each vase.

DECORATIVE VASES

When it comes to decorative vases for the home, there
are hundreds to choose from. Decorative vases are often
more expensive, but are multi-purpose as they can be
used to house a simple elegant flower arrangement or just
be displayed on their own as an ornament. I love simple
shapes and neutral colours, large white bottle-shaped
vases or curvaceous opaque glass vases that give you a chic
understated elegance but command attention, especially
when filled with a simple stem of blossom or a single
tropical leaf.

As with most displays, vases work well in groups. If you
have the space to line slightly different height vases together
or three vases that are all the same height, then this will
give more of an impact. It does not have to be expensive,
just having three vases filled with shoots of grass or a single
flower stem can often look more impressive than a
single display.

BUYING VASES

It's quite easy to find vases of good quality. Most high street
home stores offer a wide variety of practical vases of varying
sizes and quirky designs. The ideal vase is made from thick
glass, and you can test this by tapping the vase with your
fingertips. A solid noise means the glass is thick while a
little 'ting' sound means the glass may be thin in places. If
a vase is cheap, it's often for a reason. You are better off in
the long run investing in good quality glass vases that will
last you well.

Another tip is to look at the rim of the vases; if the rim is
polished and smooth then the vase will be harder to chip.
Unpolished rims are easily damaged.

adapting vases

We all love recycling and reusing something again and again. These six vases have all been covered in a different way to show you how easy it can be to adapt one yourself at home. These humble tank vases (tall rectangular vases) are the ideal vessels for all manner of coverings. Some of the items used to cover them can be found around the home, such as fabrics or ribbons.

From left to right:

Bark
The bark I have used here comes on a reel and is backed with hessian. All I've had to do to transform this vase is wrap the bark all the way around it to give a complete different look. Bark comes in many forms, most commonly as thin sheets, which are harder to bend but still workable. It is available from florists.

Snake grass
This vase has been covered with snake grass. This is a grass that resembles a snake in its appearance, bends easily and lasts for weeks out of water. Covering the vase with snake grass is a little tricky: first you need to wrap the vase in double-sided tape, then stick the snake grass onto this. I have also taped the grass down with some pot tape (see page 158) around the outside, which is then covered up with more grass over the top.

Husk
Perhaps not the easiest of things to find, but these husks work well wrapped around the tank vase. You will probably find these at your local garden centre, if not try your nearest florist, though you might have to order them in. I have just taped them down once again with double-sided tape and pot tape.

Leather
I had these silver and white leather vase-wraps specially made. We use them a lot for our corporate flower displays when we don't want people to see the water in the vase. Quite often in a hot environment such as an office, the water in vases turns dirty after just three days – these wraps help to hide this. You can make them by just getting some scrap pieces of leather and tying them around a vase with some string or leather cord.

Ribbon
This vase is a little more girly. I have simply used three different types of ribbon to transform the vase. Cut your ribbons all to the same length, then just tie them around the vase, ensuring they all overlap slightly. This takes some time, but it's very effective.

Printed fabric vase
You have to be careful when mixing fabric and flowers together, as it can often end up looking a little too much! I have chosen this off-cut of floral printed fabric that I found in a charity shop. It's a very busy fabric, so any flowers that go into this vase need to be simple – I suggest tall-stemmed pink roses to match the pink in the fabric.

For me, a house with fresh flowers is a warm and inviting home. I always try and make sure I have some kind of floral display at home, be it clean and minimal or extravagant for when I have guests. This section goes through several designs of different styles that you can use to decorate the kitchen, hallway, fireplace, bathroom and bedroom. The fishbowl and spaghetti vase arrangements show how you can achieve impact with just a few flowers, and couldn't be simpler. If you're looking for something a little more challenging, try the bathroom arrangement which has quite a masculine feel and is ideal if you're looking for a modern, architectural look. If you want to pull out all the stops, try the hallway display – a traditional front-facing arrangement with a true country garden feel. Any of these designs can be adapted with different flowers and colours, so play with my ideas to create something that complements your decor. I hope this section will show you just how quick and pain-free it can be to add a touch of colour and natural scent to your home.

flowers for the home

fishbowl

The idea here is to use the fishbowl as it was intended – a window into what's inside. By curling the flowers around the inside of the bowl, you can create a minimal, yet striking flower display that will last for well over a week.

1 Leave the calla lilies out of water for 3–5 hours. This will ensure that the stems are slightly flaccid, so that you can bend them to fit inside the fishbowl without breaking them. Fill the base of the bowl with the coloured stones. Add cold water so that the vase is half full.

flowers

10 mango calla lilies
(long stem)

other materials

Large clear glass fishbowl, approximately
30cm diameter
Coloured stones (I've used copper-
coloured chippings)

2 Cut the stems of the calla lilies at an angle so that they can drink plenty of water. Remember, they have been out of water for some time, so once they drink again they will set in the shape in which you have manipulated them. Now start gently squeezing the stems with your hands so they become supple, then simply twist the stems around the inside of the fishbowl. Place the flowers at different heights and try to disperse the heads around the vase.

Variations

Flowers for this design need to have long structural stems that can be made supple, so calla lilies and tulips are perfect. Choose long-stemmed tulips – you will need about 25 of them. Anthuriums also work well, but do not need to be left out of water beforehand, as the stems will never go supple. They will bend just enough for you to squeeze them inside the vase. You will need about nine stems.

The stones that you use at the bottom can also vary. If you have difficulty sourcing coloured stones from your local florist, try your nearest pet shop, as they often sell them to go in the bottom of fish tanks.

hallway display

For those with more traditional tastes, this front-facing hallway display creates a magnificent impression. If you are feeling extravagant or if you just want to make a statement to all who enter your home, then this is how you do it!

flowers

5 white delphiniums

15 large-headed white roses

1 bunch of rosemary

10 white freesias

5 blue hydrangeas

5 blue agapanthus

other materials

Pale blue glass bowl (a salad bowl is perfect)

1 soaked jumbo block of floral foam

Pot tape

1 Cut your floral foam to fit the inside of the bowl. The bowl I have chosen gets narrower at the bottom, so I've had to cut the floral foam to match the shape. Make sure you have plenty of room between the floral foam and the bowl to allow for water. It's also important that the floral foam is at least 5cm higher than the bowl, so you can place flowers in at an angle, coming down over the edge of the bowl. Tape the floral foam in with a tight overlapping cross of pot tape.

2 Normally you would 'green up' your display at this stage, but because this display is predominantly flowers, we are going to add our flowers straightaway. Start with the delphiniums. You need to gauge the size of the finished arrangement, so use the delphiniums as your guide. You don't want to go too wide; I suggest approximately 23cm at the sides and all around the base, and around 60cm at the top at your highest point. Delphiniums are naturally tall so focus most of these through the top of the display.

3   Add in your roses, rosemary and freesias. The flowers in this display are not grouped, so add them evenly through the display. You are aiming for a kite shape for your flowers, with a steady gradient from the top down to the bottom – almost like a pot belly. The flowers need to come out at different angles so the display looks full and shapely, not rigid and upright.

4   Finally, add in your blue hydrangeas and agapanthus. Try and focus the hydrangeas around the base. The large flower heads give weight to the arrangement and on a more practical note, keeping the stems short will help them to drink (see tips). Place the agapanthus through the centre of the design – this will bring the blue shading up through the whole display.

Tips

Hydrangeas are notorious for wilting and do not particularly like going in floral foam. Making a little slit in the base of the stem will help them to drink more.

They also need spraying with water daily, as they drink partly through their petals. This will stop the flowers from waning too quickly.

fireplace display

Encasing flowers in glass vases always gives them a contemporary feel and looks like a piece of living art. In this case, I have placed cymbidium orchids inside three spaghetti vases to give an ultra-funky look.

43

flowers

3 large green stems of cymbidium orchids

other materials

**3 tall, clear glass spaghetti vases of
different heights
Clear glass chippings
Green food colouring**

1   Tip a small amount of glass chippings into
each vase, then cover with water into which
you have stirred a few drops of green food
colouring.

2   Cut your cymbidiums so they fit easily into the
vases, then place them in, ensuring the stems are
firmly embedded into the glass chippings and
under the water.

Tips

Cymbidium orchids are fairly expensive, but they will last you on average 2–3 weeks. They
come in many colours, and are great flowers for this type of design. Try submerging the orchids
entirely under water – just leave out the food colouring. You get a wonderful magnified effect.
Anthuriums, calla lilies and tulips can also be submerged in this way – although tulips won't last
as long. Food colouring will not harm your flowers; it's a simple, but effective tool for changing
the look of any vase display.

Flowers don't have to be pretty and girly; this display of chocolate anthuriums bound onto dark sugar canes would sit proudly in even the most masculine of environments. This is one of those displays designed to create a reaction.

bathroom

1 Firstly, you need to fill your phials with water, then cover with the black tie leaves. Cut the black tie leaves in half, place each phial onto a black tie leaf and wrap this around, binding with the coloured wire.

2 Cut down nine of your anthuriums and place them into the covered phials. Make sure the stems are deep down inside the phials and leave about 5cm of stem coming out at the top. Leave the other two anthuriums with long stems; these can be placed straight into the vase.

flowers

11 chocolate anthuriums

9 sugar canes

5 black tie leaves

(cordyline leaves)

other materials

9 water phials

Reel of coloured wire

Household sticky tape

Medium-height grey vase

Tips

Phials come in handy when you are trying to create height with short-stemmed flowers. They are also great for creating large displays where you can't have all the flowers in water.

You may find that not all your anthuriums will need cutting down and placing in phials. If their stems are long, then simply place them straight into the vase. This also gives some variation to the arrangement.

3 Add water to the vase, then create a grid over the top using the sticky tape. Place your sugar canes in between the gaps in the grid. The idea of the grid is to keep the stems separated and stop them from falling to one side.

4 Bind each covered phial and anthurium onto the sugar cane with the coloured wire. You will need to bind the phials in two places: the top and the bottom. This will prevent them from tilting under the weight of the anthuriums. Try to disperse the flowers evenly through the sugar canes. Place the two single anthuriums in the front of the arrangement.

bedroom bud vases

Set the mood in the bedroom with these delicate blooms arranged in miniature glass bottles and vases. There is something about waking up next to a little vase of flowers. You can use any small vessel, from a drinking glass to a cup and saucer.

Notes

A bud vase is one which holds a single flower stem. Bud vases, such as the ones shown opposite, come in many shapes and sizes – perfect for showing off a single rose or gerbera.

My grandmother has always had flowers dotted around her house in mini vases, and now I can see why; they lift the mood and bring life into the home.

flowers

A selection of same-colour flowers, such as roses, gerberas, nerines and alstroemerias

other materials

A selection of bottles in different shapes and sizes, and bud vases

How often throughout the year do we receive flowers? Probably two or three times: once on a birthday, once on Mother's Day and, if you are lucky, on Valentine's Day. Flowers can say it all when words fail you. They can remind us that we are loved, they show us people care, and they even have their own language, with many flowers having historic meanings and symbols that most of us are unaware of. So with flowers epitomising so much, it's easy to see what amazing gifts they make. These gifts become even more unique when made by yourself – anything we create ourselves has more meaning, making the gift extra special. Over the next few pages, you will discover how to make your own hand-tied bouquets and wrap them; you will learn how to construct a gift wrap of flowers; and for something unusual and the ultimate floral gift, I have demonstrated a hatbox flower display.

flowers as gifts

A gorgeous compact posy of pure flowers is almost more romantic as a gift than any other. What we often get from men is 'as big as we can get for our money', but in all truth a sweet compact bouquet with thought behind it like this one can say a lot more.

compact hand-tied
bouquet

flowers

6 white Avalanche roses

9 white lilacs

8 white agapanthus

20 white freesias

other materials

Floristry string

1 square metre sheet of clear cellophane

6 sheets of white tissue paper

Ribbon

1 Cut all of your stems to approximately 38cm in length – this will make the flowers easier to work with. Then begin by grouping all of your flower types together in groups of three for the roses and lilacs, and groups of four for the agapanthus and freesias.

2 Group them by spiralling them together (so all the stems are facing the same way, much like spaghetti in a spaghetti jar) and tie them all at the same point, approximately one hand's length from the bottom of the flowers.

3 Start to add the bunched flowers together, ensuring you continue to spiral. Hold in one place and surround each group with different flower groups. It's very important that you hold the stems in the exact same place throughout the entire process. Holding stems lower will create a larger bouquet, whereas holding them higher (in this case, one hand's length from the start of the flower heads) will give you a more compact bouquet.

4 Continue to add all of your flower groups in no particular order, ensuring they are all well mixed in among each other. Remember to have them all sitting at the same height to give you the perfect dome shape at the end. Once all your flowers are added, bind with floristry string and tie in the exact same place you have been holding the bouquet.

5 Follow the steps on page 60 for wrapping in cellophane and tissue paper. Finish by tying with ribbon.

Tips

Spiralling your flowers is very important. If all the stems are going in the same direction, they all find their own space. When stems start to cross, they are in conflict with each other, and this can result in soft stems being squashed by harder stems when you tie the bouquet at the end. Spiralling also looks neater once the flowers are in the vase.

Rosie

loose hand-tied bouquet

This magnificent country-style bouquet is the ultimate gift for when words are hard to find. We don't receive flowers that often through the year, so why not put the bouquet together yourself and make it extra special.

flowers

2 antique pink hydrangeas

8 pink roses

8 stems of hypericum berries

5 pink alstroemerias

5 bouvardias

10 stems of salal tips

10 stems of senecio

other materials

1 square metre sheet of clear cellophane

Floristry string

6 sheets of brown tissue paper

1 metre length of ribbon

loose hand-tied bouquets

This bouquet is made in much the same way as the white compact hand-tied bouquet on page 54. The only real difference here is that you hold the stems slightly lower when constructing the bouquet. In doing this, you will find the flowers spread out more and fill a larger space. This will give you a looser and taller bouquet.

1 Place your bouquet upright in the middle of the square sheet of clear cellophane, ensuring the cellophane is even on all four sides.

2 Bring the sides of the cellophane up to meet your bouquet, at the tie point. Once the stems are completely covered with the cellophane, tightly tie with floristry string. Your tie point should be directly over the top of your holding point and previous tie point.

3 Take two sheets of tissue paper and line them up on top of each other. Hold the two sheets together at the top corners. Gently start to scrunch the tissue paper at one corner to bring it up, while pulling the paper tightly at the other corner to crease into a concertina style. This will give you a large fan of tissue paper. Make three of these fans.

4 Once all three are made, place them around the edge of the bouquet. Don't go too wide – the last thing you want is a bouquet where all you can see is the wrapping and not the flowers. I would aim to place the middle of the fans over your tie point. Overlap the fans and pleat together, then tie with a piece of ribbon.

gift wrap

Here the gift wrap has been given a modern update with black cellophane and simple structural flowers. Gift wraps give the recipient the chance to arrange the flowers themselves, as opposed to hand-ties which can be put straight into a vase.

flowers

8 stems of bells of Ireland

6 stems of tuberose

6 shamrock chrysanthemums

3 stems of snake grass

other materials

1.5 square metre sheet of black cellophane

10 sheets of brown tissue paper

1 metre of ribbon

1 Lay your cellophane out flat on your work surface. Make a fan from a double layer of tissue paper. Fan the paper by scrunching at one end and pulling tight at the other. Lay it in the top-left-hand corner of the cellophane and make sure the tissue paper sits neatly on top of the cellophane with no overlapping sides – this will help to keep things tidy. Lay three stems of bells of Ireland directly on top of the tissue paper all at even intervals. Allow the flower stems to overhang the edge of the tissue paper slightly.

2 Make another double tissue-paper fan and lay this directly on top of the flowers, this time placing the fan slightly lower down so you can see the flowers underneath. Add your grass to one side of the display, then add three stems of tuberose. Add another double layer of tissue paper, once again placing this slightly lower down.

3 Now add a few more stems of bells of Ireland and three stems of shamrock chrysanthemums, ensuring everything is evenly placed. Place the shamrock heads just below the end of the tissue paper. Add a further double fan of brown tissue paper and add your remaining flower stems.

4 Once all your flowers are added, place a final double fan of tissue paper over the stems of the last flowers. Bring the cellophane up and over the whole design so it covers the entire front of the display. Wrap the cellophane around the back and bind with ribbon at the point where all the flower stems cross.

Variation

You don't always have to use cellophane and tissue paper when it comes to gift-wrapping flowers. For a softer, more elegant look, use coordinating fabric (see page 62). I've wrapped these paper whites (which smell divine!) in two-tone frayed green fabric. I've used green ribbon to bind and added a little crystal droplet with a black gift card to make this very simple bunch of flowers extra special. You can use many other fabrics and materials for this – even newspaper print and recycled papers.

A great alternative to the common hand-tied bouquet or gift wrap, the hatbox display offers a quirky take on combining fashion and flowers. It is ideal to give to anyone who appreciates something a little different.

hatbox

1 Soak your floral foam (see page 165). Meanwhile, line the hatbox with cellophane. Place the floral foam on one side of the lined hatbox, and stuff the other side with cellophane – you don't need the whole hatbox to be filled with floral foam. Stuffing half the space with a mass of scrunched-up cellophane helps keep the weight and, importantly, the cost down.

2 Insert a cut stem into the floral foam to help hold the hatbox lid at an angle, allowing for a large gap to be filled with flowers. Cut away any excess cellophane. Now you have your container ready it's time to start filling it with foliage and a mass of summery blooms. I have chosen some of my favourite summer plants here: roses, hydrangeas, mint and sage. All the flowers I have chosen are available at the same time of year and are toned together in colour.

flowers

12 Old Dutch roses

2 large antique pink hydrangeas

10 stems of mint

1 bunch of garden sage

other materials

1 block of floral foam

Hatbox

1 square metre sheet of cellophane

5 wired strands of pearls

5 wired pieces of lace

Ribbon

See page 170 for instructions on how to
wire the lace and pearls. Use 0.90mm gage
wire or thereabouts.

Note

3 Cut all your flower and foliage stems roughly to the same length; this will make them easier to work with. Wire your pearls and lace (see page 158). Much as for a chef, preparation is everything when it comes to flower arranging! Take your foliage and fill the open side of the hatbox with a domed mass, placing the stems deep into the floral foam. Each stem of foliage should be even with the next – you don't want stray leaves poking up where not wanted.

4 Now simply fill the open side of the hatbox with a mass of your chosen flowers, ensuring that all the stems are secure in the floral foam and that all the flower heads are positioned at the same height throughout the display. Use wired lace and pearls to finish (see picture on page 67) and tie a bow around the hatbox to complete.

rose
cubes

Perfect for a little thank you, these rose cubes would brighten up anyone's day!
A simple idea presented beautifully, it just goes to show you how easy it is to create
something unique that can be used for all manner of occasions.

flowers

9 Grand Prix roses

other materials

13cm clear glass cube vase
Soaked block of floral foam
1.5 metres of ribbon

1 Cut your soaked floral foam into a small section, approximately 2.5cm thick and 10cm square, to fit into the base of your cube vase. (See tip on covering the foam). Cut your roses down so each rose has a stem that's 13cm in length.

2 Place your roses into the floral foam in lines of three until you have filled the whole vase with flowers. Ensure the rose heads sit just above the top of the cube vase.

3 Fill with water and tie a piece of ribbon around the cube as you would a gift.

Tips

Tulips, dahlias and peonies are other flowers to use in this way. Nutans, water lilies and agapanthus will give much the same look but offer a more contemporary style. Water lilies in particular are more expensive, so these would be suited for a special occasion.

If you are using a clear glass vase, cover the base with stones or glass chippings – you don't want to see the floral foam! Ideally, however, you could use a coloured vase – black is best for red roses. Use other coloured cube vases and coordinate with the colour of your flowers.

Variation

To make a display with slightly more height, you can arrange the roses into a small hand-tied bouquet (see picture below and on page 70). Cut the rose stems down so they are approximately 18cm in length and simply bunch them together with 3 or 4 sprigs of berried ivy or garden sage, and a few galax leaves, as you would a hand-tied bouquet (see page 54).

Once the mini bouquet is made, cut the stems again so the posy fits into the cube, with the roses heads sitting just above the rim of the vase. Don't forget to fill with water.

There really is no excuse these days for leaving plants sitting in the plastic plant pots they came in! We can all do much better than that. I have planted these five different varieties of echeveria in simple glass containers that are readily available on the high

plants in different containers

street. The one at the end in the fishbowl has been planted with a covering of clear glass stones. These gifts would make a suitable moving-in present, and as these plants don't mind hot environments, you could give them away as an office desk plant.

1 If your plant is too big for the fishbowl in its plastic pot, then remove the plastic pot and any excess soil. Cover the soil with cellophane or clingfilm to help keep the soil together and prevent too much water leaking out. Add a few stones to the base of the fishbowl, so that the plant will sit above the rim of the bowl when it is placed inside.

2 Place the echeveria inside the bowl, and have the plant sitting just on the rim of the vase. Then carefully begin to add your glass chippings around the edge of the plant. You might find it easier to use a small cup to do this. Ensure the stones are evenly distributed around the inside of the fishbowl, and remember to check for any gaps.

plants

1 small echeveria plant in its pot

other materials

1 small clear glass fishbowl

Small sheet of cellophane or clingfilm

1 bag of clear glass chippings

Note

When watering, pour water right into the heart of the plant. All it needs is half an eggshell of water every couple of weeks.

For a relaxed gathering at home, a more formal affair or just for the sheer hell of it, this section will show you just what's needed to create the perfect party centrepieces. This is probably the only chance I get to arrange flowers at home where I put plenty of effort into what I'm doing. You just know that your guests are going to comment on your work and flatter you. When I'm arranging flowers for a dinner party, I try to keep it relatively simple – that's not to say I compromise on the impact. The following pages are filled with clever ideas and effective designs that you can easily replicate at home. Have fun cracking open some ostrich eggs for an Easter table, let your eccentric side show with a Mad Hatter-inspired garden tea party or just relax and unwind with an informal planted table display. My favourite and indeed the best-selling table centre we produce at Jamie Aston is the candelabra. This type of display gives you height and impact with plenty of candlelight – ideal for any occasion.

party flowers

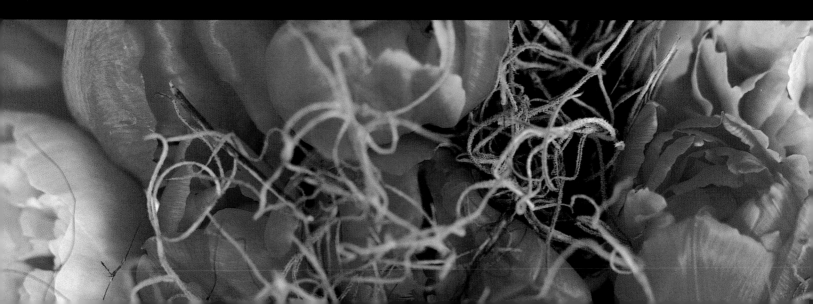

spring table

I can't imagine this display going unnoticed in anyone's home. This spring table is such a playful arrangement your friends won't fail to comment. I have used ostrich eggs here to create an interesting display, but you could also use small bowls.

1 Your ostrich eggs should be pre-blown; if you wanted to you could try doing this yourself but I would not recommend it! You need to break the eggs in half. This is a little tricky and if you can't crack them then take a kitchen knife or saw and try to prise them apart. I used a saw to make my first cut and then I managed to pull the egg open from there.

2 Cut your flower foam into mini blocks to fit inside half of your hollow eggs. The foam needs to sit either level with the edge of the egg or a little higher. You could place pot tape over the foam now and secure it into place inside the egg, but these eggs are just going to sit on a table, so I don't think this is completely necessary.

flowers

15 viburnum

50 yellow ranunculus

other materials

1 soaked block of flower foam

4 blown ostrich eggs

Pot tape (optional)

3 Cut all of your viburnum down to lengths of approximately 8cm. Now begin to fill the foam-filled eggs with the viburnum. The stems should be firmly embedded in the flower foam – viburnum is not one of the best drinkers so this will help. Ensure the whole egg is full and that you have no gaps.

4 Now cut down all of your ranunculus to the same length and begin to fill these through the viburnum into the flower foam. Once you have filled all of your eggs that have the foam, you will need to arrange them into an uneven pile in the centre of your table together with the empty egg halves. You might find placing some double-sided tape to the bottom of the eggs will help them stay in place. Also see Table Settings on page 95.

Tip

If you can't find ostrich eggs you could make your own with papier-mâché. Take a small balloon and cover with papier-mâché. This will give you an egg shape. Once this has dried, break in half and use as you would the ostrich eggs. You may need to line the papier-mâché eggs with some cellophane to stop them from getting wet.

rustic dinner party

This casual setting shows how you can make the most of plants on the dinner table. It is a simple design that will last for weeks, smell divine and, most importantly, impress your friends.

They can be made way in advance then pulled together for your dinner party. Chive grass and steel grass are two alternatives to the blue fescue grass shown here, but bear in mind that grasses are difficult to maintain like this, because they're essentially outdoor plants. Have them in containers on your patio and bring them inside when you need them.

85

flowers

8 blue hyacinth bulbs

3 blue fescue grasses

other materials

1 box of flat moss

5 mirrored glass cube vases

1 To plant the hyacinths, first fill two glass cubes one third of the way up with moss to help raise the height of the hyacinth bulbs. Then place four hyacinth bulbs in their plastic containers inside each cube next to each other and cover with more moss.

2 Take the grasses out of their pots and place them straight into the remaining glass cubes, then cover the soil on show with moss.

Tip

These displays will need watering twice a week with approximately 200ml of water. Be careful not to overwater the grasses, as they do not have any drainage in these glass cubes. If you like, you could also try mind-your-own-business, an attractive, low-maintenance indoor plant.

contemporary
dinner party

It does not get much easier than this clean and minimal design. Here it's all about using the right vases – in this case several tall spaghetti vases. Use same-colour flowers of different heights and textures, and vary the water level in each vase. I've covered the bases of the vases with bark, which comes on a roll from florists and just wraps around the vase and tapes into place.

flowers

3 stems of lilac
6 white roses
10 stems of pussy willow
5 calla lilies

other materials

5 tall clear glass spaghetti vases
1 reel of bark
Pot tape

Tips

Use roses with stems of different lengths – floating a rose head in a vase filled two thirds up with water looks very effective.

Calla lilies and arums don't like to be placed in too much water; they start to decay faster and often turn to mush.

formal dinner party

This stunning long and low table centrepiece will allow your guests to communicate with each other without the flowers dominating their view. I have chosen deep reds and burgundies here for a rich, luxurious feel, along with some unusual items, such as chillies and brassicas, to give a quirky look to this formal display.

The chillies and brassicas I've used are purposely grown for florists; they both come on long stems. You can use normal chillies, but you'd have to wire them to add length (see page 170).

flowers

3 bunches of eucalyptus, 18 Grand Prix roses, 12 pink brassicas,

10 red chillies, 30 deep burgundy ranunculus

other materials

2 soaked blocks of floral foam, 2 floral foam trays, pot tape,

5 bunches of fake-frosted red grapes or fresh red grapes (see

page 94 on how to frost fresh grapes)

1 Place each soaked floral foam onto a tray – they should fit perfectly. Bind the floral foam tightly onto the trays at both ends using pot tape. This will add a backbone to the display. Place your two trays together in a line.

2 Start adding in the eucalyptus. It's best if you have your foliage cut to the ideal length before you start. This stage is very important, as the scale of the design will be dictated by the foliage. You are aiming for a height of approximately 13cm around the edges and 20cm on top.

3 At various intervals, add in clusters of roses and brassicas, ideally in groups of three, and remember to push your stems deep into the floral foam. Add the chillies and bunches of grapes through the design. Most fake grape bunches come pre-wired. Otherwise (or if you are using fresh grapes), refer to page 170 for wiring instructions.

4 Finally, add in your ranunculus in clusters of three or five. Ranunculus have soft stems, so you may find it a little difficult getting these into the floral foam. Hold them right at the bottom of the stem and tease them in. You can also make a small dent in the floral foam with a pen to give yourself a guide hole and a head start.

table settings

Why not spruce up your table with a few extra finishing touches? These simple and easy ideas are a foolproof way of jazzing up any dinner table. I hate seeing a flower display just dumped in the middle; it takes more than that to create a setting and address the mood. By simply laying a flower on a napkin, you automatically bring the floral display at the centre out to all your guests.

2 For a fresh and more contemporary look, I have placed this glass plate on top of an aralia leaf. These leaves are large and flat so are great for place mats. I have also wrapped some bark around the glass plate itself to add further detail. This place setting would be ideal for the contemporary dinner party on page 88.

1 Here I have used some artificial sugar-coated grapes as a prop to hold a place setting. The frosted grapes stand out against the white linen and the name tag is made from eucalyptus leaves. I've just tied these onto the grapes with blue ribbon. If you want to use real grapes, you would need to dip them in egg white followed by caster sugar to get the same effect. A good idea for the formal dinner party on page 90.

3 This elegant burgundy calla lily has been cut short and placed diagonally across a china plate. I have wrapped gold ribbon around the plate as if it were a parcel and tucked the printed napkin under the bow. It's such a stylish look, just the thing for when you want to impress at a formal dinner party (see page 90).

4 A slightly frosted pear is the perfect stage for this name card. Placed in a glass bowl, it looks almost like a dessert. The pear has been dipped in egg white and caster sugar. I have torn a luggage tag into a name card and attached this by placing the hole in the tag over the stem of the pear. For a more festive feel, I have arranged some pine around the base of the bowl – this would be lovely for a Christmas table.

5 For an Easter-inspired table setting, these egg shells with yellow ranunculus flowers resting inside do the trick. It's almost like little chicks hatching out! Duck eggs, which tend to be paler in colour, would work equally well. This would look great with the spring table on page 80.

garden party

This cake stand displays cupcake cases full of flowers. I've dusted icing sugar over them to give a more authentic feel and stacked crockery from a charity shop on the table. The look is very much Mad Hatter's Tea Party – great for a summer gathering!

1 Cut your floral foam into mini blocks to fit the silver cupcake cases, then cut all of your flower stems down to approximately 2.5–5cm.

2 Fill the cupcake cases with sweet peas or hydrangea heads, ensuring all the stems are secured within the floral foam. Break up your hydrangea heads, so they go further.

3 If you want to go for the vintage look, spray your hydrangea heads with a dusting of gold spray paint. It does not kill the flowers straightaway, so this will be fine for an event or party. I have just sprayed my heads very lightly; you don't want to overdo it.

4 I have covered my flowers with icing sugar to add a touch of authenticity. Simply sprinkle the icing sugar over the flowers when you have them in position – it's always nice to get some on the table and make a bit of a mess. Assemble the flowers onto the cake stand and surround it with odd bits of crockery. I have used an old teapot, a few cups and saucers and a sugar pot to float a few roses, cornflowers and hydrangea heads. Sprinkle the whole thing with more icing sugar and you're done. (Don't try too hard with this one; it is supposed to look disorganised and natural, just chuck it all together and have fun!)

flowers

5 large lilac hydrangea heads

30 sweet peas, in mixed pinks and lilacs

9 pink roses

9 cornflowers

other materials

1 soaked block of floral foam

15 silver cupcake cases

Gold spray paint

Icing sugar

Three-tier cake stand

Mixed vintage crockery

Candelabras are one of the most popular designs for weddings and parties – they sit well on any table. Their stems are tall and thin, so you can see across the table, yet you have a mass of stunning flowers and candles. I have kept this one very simple.

candelabra

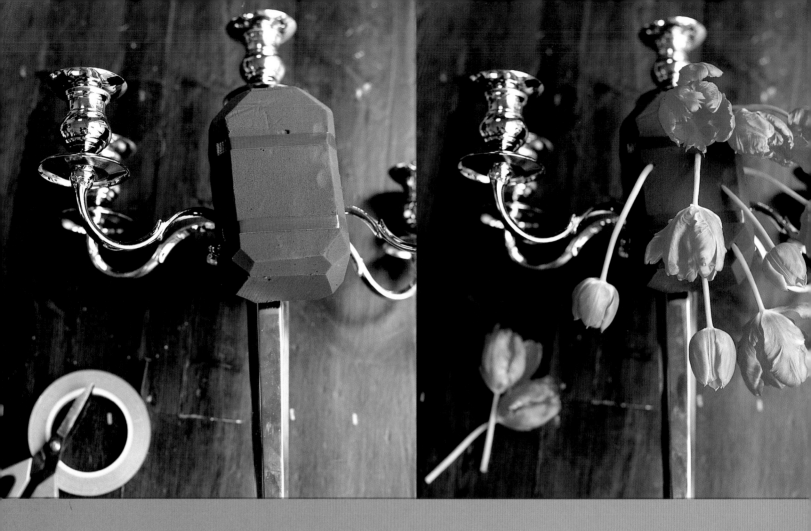

1   Mitre the edges of your floral foam blocks by shaving away with a knife. By doing this, you will find it easier to place flower stems into the floral foam at the edges. Place the floral foam blocks centrally on the candelabra's arms on each side and secure with pot tape.

Notes

You would normally wrap the floral foam in chicken wire before securing to the candelabra. This just helps give the foam more strength for when it is filled with lots of flower stems. In this case, we do not have many heavy flowers going through, so for a quick fix this method will be absolutely fine.

2   Your tulips, if open, will have a natural bend in their stems. Cut them down to 25cm. Add the tulips evenly through the floral foam, with the curve in the stem naturally cascading outwards and down – you want to have them coming out approximately 15–20cm from the floral foam. The flower heads should not extend beyond the outer candelabra arms, and the shape you are aiming for is that of a ball, the size of a large melon.

Tip

Tulips stems can be quite soft, so if you find it hard getting them into the floral foam, then use the end of a pen to make a little guide hole in the floral foam for your tulips.

3 Now cut your peonies down to approximately 25cm and begin to add these by dotting them through the tulips in little clusters of two or three. Ensure you pay attention to the underside of the candelabra, the part which people will be looking at from the table. It's very easy to forget about this section and focus on the sides and top. Also remember to try and keep all of your flower heads at the same height; you don't want any coming out too far and overshadowing the rest.

4 Finally, add your Spanish moss. This is great stuff; just pull it out of the bag and play with it in your hand before adding it into the display. I have just tucked the moss into any gaps I could see in my candelabra. Let the moss do what it wants, so you have these trails coming down. The moss gives the candelabra a whole different look – it makes it seem almost vintage-like, as if it has just been pulled out of the attic. Spanish moss, and indeed any kind of moss, is great for filling in gaps and hiding your mechanics.

flowers

50 fully open vivid pink double tulips

20 fully open soft pink peonies

1 box of Spanish moss

other materials

2 soaked blocks of floral foam

1 tall five-armed candelabra

Pot tape

I can't think of anything more special than creating your friend's wedding flowers yourself. As daunting as this sounds, it really is, like everything else in this book, quite simple. The trick here as always is not to panic and just enjoy yourself. Most of the trends in wedding flowers come down the line from the bridal dress designers, so bear this in mind and use the bride's gown as your inspiration. This chapter includes a beautiful compact rose bouquet entwined with pearls and crystals – perfect with a vintage dress. You will also learn how to make an elegant trailing vivid pink orchid bouquet, a style that can be easily adapted using your own chosen flowers. My personal favourites in this chapter are the bridesmaid's pomander and flower handbag, which offer something different for the modern bridal party. The handbag, bizarre as it may sound, is very popular with little girls who seem to cherish it much more than an ordinary bouquet. Finally, the buttonholes are a great introduction to wiring and you will be amazed at how easy they are to make.

wedding flowers

I'm not suggesting for a second that you make your own wedding bouquet – apparently that would be bad luck! But if you get the chance to make one for a friend, this project will help. It's a compact posy made with vintage roses and pearls.

compact posy

1 Firstly, condition your roses so that there are no leaves or thorns left on any of the stems, then cut all of your rose stems down to about 38cm in length – this makes them easier to work with. Wire your diamanté and pearl clusters onto half the roses. All you need to do here is place the cluster just in between the top rose petals, bring the wire down through the rose head and wrap this around the stem. The clusters need to be as subtle as possible, so don't have them protruding too far out the top.

2 Your next step will be to construct the bouquet. This is much like the compact hand-tied bouquet on pages 56 and 57. Hold the stems as high as you can, approximately 8cm from the head of the roses. Keeping your hand in the same place will ensure that the bouquet remains compact. Spiral all of your stems into place, adding in one rose with a wired diamanté or pearl and then one without, to ensure they are evenly spread. Bind with pot tape. If you prefer, you can bind the bouquet as you make it, which will help keep its shape and make it a little easier.

flowers

20 vintage roses

other materials

5 wired diamanté clusters, 5 wired pearl clusters, pot tape, 1 metre length of coordinating ribbon, pearl-headed pins, 2 strands of pearls

3 Now you need to add your ribbon. I always start by placing one end of the ribbon over my binding point (where you have tied the bouquet). You can either pin this down with a pearl-headed pin or tape it with pot tape. Once one end is secure, pull the ribbon tight and wrap this around the stems approximately three or four times. Then make three little loops with your ribbon and pin the final loop down, ensuring the pin goes through the other two loops and into the rose stems to secure.

4 Finally, I have added a few strands of pearls around my binding point. This just adds a little something extra to the whole design. Quite often we match bridal bouquets to the bridal dress; if a bride is wearing a gown covered in beading, then this would complement her dress perfectly. You can pin the strands of pearls down with one or two pearl-headed pins, which will just blend in. Finish by cutting your stems down to 20–25cm.

Tips

Brides always want to learn of ways to keep their bouquets. Freeze-drying is an option where someone comes and collects the bouquet immediately after the wedding, but it is very expensive. Rather, dry the bouquet upside-down in a cool, dry place. It will lose shape and the heads will shrink, so just rearrange it after a while.

Notes

I have used Equadorian Peppermint roses for this posy. Other vintage-style roses are Metallina, Illusion and Old Dutch.

Variation

This delightful country-style posy is constructed in much the same way as the bridal rose bouquet (see page 108). There are more varieties of flowers and a lot more stems, but the mechanics behind the display are really very similar.

I have used fragrant blue muscari with blue hyacinths and lilacs here with a small amount of salal foliage. The flowers all work incredibly well together; they all have the same textures and delightful fragrances. I have bound this posy slightly differently with coordinating satin ribbon fastened down with a line of crystal-headed pins.

One drawback to this bouquet is that it won't dry as easily as the rose posy. If you wanted to preserve it after a wedding, you would have to get it done professionally.

flowers

35 pale blue muscari

5 stems of lilac

10 blue hyacinths

5 stems of salal tips

10 galax leaves

other materials

1 metre length of lilac satin ribbon

12 pearl- or crystal-headed pins

You don't always have to stick to white for wedding flowers. These stunning phalaenopsis orchids make the perfect trailing bouquet, and it's so easy! The butterflies add a magical touch to the design, far from the ordinary.

trailing pink
orchid bouquet

1 Place your orchid stems together, so that all of the heads are facing the same way. Take your longest stem first and add the smaller stems around this one. Once you have them all in the right place, with all the heads facing the same way and a natural curve in the trail of the orchids, bind the stems together with gutter tape.

2 Now add your steel grass behind the orchids, so it backs the display and trails through the stems in and among the orchid heads. Bind this onto the orchid stems with more gutter tape. Wire the butterflies around the grass at different intervals through the bouquet. I have placed three of them through my bouquet: one at the top, one in the middle and one towards the end of the trail.

3 Finally, bind some lilac or hot pink ribbon around the stems and attach this with two decorative pins. You could tie this into a bow, but I find pinning ribbon down a lot neater. It also gives you the opportunity to add a touch of sparkle.

flowers

3 stems of large hot pink phalaenopsis orchids
1 bunch of steel grass

other materials

Gutter tape
3 wired iridescent butterflies
0.5 metre of lilac or hot pink ribbon
2 decorative pins

Variations

trailing tulip bouquet

Trailing bouquets can come in many forms, and this yellow tulip bouquet is elegant and vibrant. Tulips trail best when they are left out of water for several hours – their stems become limp and bendy, making them the perfect flower for this type of bouquet.

I have wrapped the stems with variegated tulip leaves here and finished off with my trademark pearls!

flowers

25 yellow tulips with variegated leaves
2 bunches of bear grass

other materials

2 strands of pearls
Pearl-headed pins

trailing arum lily bouquet

For a more traditional, almost 1930s-style trailing bouquet, these glorious white arum lilies are perfect. You need to leave the stems out of water for several hours before they start to become supple. I have added some bear grass to these arums just to help lift the design. If you like, you could thread beads or crystals onto the bear grass. This is an easy way to add a touch of glamour.

flowers

9 large arum lilies
1 bunch of bear grass
2 alocasia leaves

other materials

20 pearl-headed pins

headdress

These look great on young bridesmaids or flower girls. I think they are best suited to children, as adults require something more sophisticated. I'm not a great fan of masses of flowers in the hair, but a pretty headdress can look sweet on the right head.

pomander

Pomanders are small- to medium-sized balls of flowers often with ribbon handles.
Little bridesmaids treasure these more than the usual hand-tied posy. This one is made
from soft pink ranunculus with a pearl handle and pearls dotted through.

headdress

1 Start by making the frame. Gutter tape the two 0.90mm wires together. The length that you make these into will depend on the size of the bridesmaid's head. Use a piece of string to measure. Create a loop at one end and a hook at the other. Just bend the wires into a loop and tape this down with gutter tape. Make the hook by just bending the wires.

2 Now go through your spray roses and cut off all the larger heads and some of the closed buds. Wire all of the heads as illustrated in Tools and Techniques (see page 166) – I've used 0.28mm and 0.44mm gage wires as the flowers are quite small in this project. Cut your lilacs and bouvardia into smaller pieces – try and make them all the same size, each piece with a stem. Wire the flowers by placing the wire next to the stem and secure in the normal way outlined in the Tools and Techniques section.

flowers

5 stems of spray pink roses, 2 stems of lilacs, 5 stems of bouvardia

other materials

Gutter tape, 2 x 0.90mm gage wires, 20 x 0.28mm gage wires, 20 x 0.44mm gage wires

3 Once all of your flowers are wired and sealed, you can start to add them onto the frame to construct the headdress. I have made my headdress with all of the flowers evenly spread through the design. You might choose to place the smaller flowers, such as the buds, towards the ends and focus the larger headed flowers towards the middle of the headdress. Attach each flower by laying the flower and its wires directly onto the frame, then gutter tape these together. Continue this pattern with an even mix of flowers and head sizes. You will need to have the flower heads facing either side of the frame, so when you lay one rose with its head facing left, you then need to lay the next flower either in the middle or facing right.

 4 The headdress will become thicker with wires as you go along; keep taping as you go, ensuring all the wires remain flat and in line with the frame. Once you get to the end of the frame and all of your flowers are securely wired, cut any overhang and excess wires neatly at an angle and gutter tape these down. They will be very hard to cut, but it's important there are no sharp bits of wire poking through.

pomander

1 Carve your soaked floral foam block into a small ball, roughly the size of an apple, using a floristry knife – take care not to squash the floral foam too much. Now you need to make and secure your handle. Double up your pearl strands, cut them to approximately 30cm in length, then attach an 0.44mm wire to either end of the pearl strands by simply winding the wire around the pearls. Gutter tape the wires right to the end. The gutter tape will help prevent the wires from rusting, thus preventing any damage to white dresses!

2 Take your pearl handle and push the wires through the centre of the ball. Once they are out the other end, bring the wires up and around the outside to meet the entry hole. Then just bind these wires around each other and cut off the excess.

3 Cut all of your ranunculus to approximately 4cm in length. Then cut the gage wires into 5cm lengths. Place a 5cm length of gage wire up into the stem of each ranunculus leaving approximately 2.5cm of the wire showing at the end of the stem. Because ranunculus have soft stems, wiring them in this way will make it easier for you to push them into the floral foam. Begin adding your flowers into the floral foam – you may wish to hang the pomander on the back of a chair, so that you can access it all around. I always start with a cross, so place one flower into each side to begin.

4 Now fill in the gaps between your cross of flowers – it's very important that all the stems are tightly held in the floral foam and that all of the flower heads are at the same level. This will give you that perfect ball shape. Once all the flowers are secured and you're happy with the general shape of your pomander, add in the large pearl-headed pins. Place these evenly through the pomander. Let the pomander hang for 30 minutes or so, just to allow the water to drip out of the floral foam.

Tips

Some people like to wrap the floral foam ball in mini chicken wire to help keep the ball from falling apart. Feel free to do this, but I have never found this to be of any great use.

flowers

40 pale pink ranunculus (Italian)

other materials

$\frac{1}{2}$ a soaked block of floral foam, strands of pearls,
22 x 0.44mm gage wires, gutter tape, 10 long,
large pearl-headed pins

flower
handbag

I love these miniature flower handbags. They won't fail to attract attention, but the detailing is key and you need to have plenty of patience for it. This one is made from individual hyacinth pips, so not only does it look sweet, it smells sweet too.

1 Shape your floral foam into a miniature handbag by carving around the top of the block and down the sides, keeping the bottom of the floral foam flat. Carve any corners off so that the floral foam is rounded at the top. Tape around the foam with a cross of pot tape. Wire each end of the pearl strand with 0.71mm gage wire.

2 Push the handle wires through the floral foam and twist them over the pot tape to secure and prevent them from slipping back inside and falling out. Cut off any excess. Start to remove the hyacinth pips from the stems; just pick them off one by one, choosing all the open ones that are at their best.

flowers

10 fully open pink hyacinths, 8 galax leaves

other materials

$\frac{1}{2}$ a soaked block of floral foam, pot tape, 25cm strand of large pearls, 2 x 0.71mm gage wires, 100 x 0.28mm gage wires, diamanté-headed pins, pearl-headed pins, 1 brooch

Variation

If you don't have the time to wire hyacinth pips, use spray roses instead. These don't need to be wired as their stems can be stuck straight into the floral foam. This handbag also makes a great gift for grown-up girls, whichever flowers you use!

3 Cut the 0.28mm gage wires into 5cm lengths. Take each length and wire them though the bottom part of the hyacinth pips, then bend the ends together. Place them into the floral foam, working from the bottom upwards (leaving the back and bottom for the galax leaves) and ensuring they are all at the same level and all as open as each other – if you have any closed pips, try to mix these in with all the open ones. The pips do not go into the floral foam themselves; as long as the wire is firmly in, they will be secure.

4 For the clasp, place lots of pearl-headed pins into the floral foam in the shape of a bag opening. Attach your brooch in the middle. (If the brooch has no pin of its own, pin it into the floral foam using the pearl-headed pins.)

5 Now you need to cover the back and bottom of your handbag. It would be a waste of time placing hyacinth pips in these areas, so I have used little galax leaves. Cut the leaves off their stems and pin them onto the back and bottom of the handbag with diamanté- or pearl-headed pins. Try and get the leaves neatly lined up and pin them evenly to prevent the bag looking messy.

buttonholes

Buttonholes are slightly overlooked and are often constructed from carnations, but they don't have to be drab and uninspiring. The rose buttonhole is one of the most popular choices, but if you want to stand out, why not add in some wired pearls?

1 Cut the rose head at an angle, approximately 1–2cm from the base. Do the same with the ivy, leaving 3cm of stem. Wire the rose head and ivy leaves (see pages 166 and 168).

2 Wind gutter tape over the wires. Bind the taped stems together with more gutter tape, so that the ivy leaves are framing the rose. You may want to add two or three ivy leaves in here, depending on the size of buttonhole you are going for. Cut all the wires down to 6cm and gutter tape right to the end.

3 Make this extra special by covering your taped wires with a coordinating piece of ribbon. Simply back a strand of ribbon with some double-sided tape and wrap this around the wired stems. Add your pearl-headed pin and you're done. A simple, yet elegant wired buttonhole.

flowers

Rose head, ivy leaves

other materials

0.44mm gage wire, 0.56mm gage wire, 0.28mm gage wire, gutter tape, coordinating ribbon, double-sided tape, pearl-headed pin

Variations

You could cover the rose head with iridescent glitter. Simply mist the rose with spray glue and dip the head into a mound of glitter. This will frame the edge of the petals and give you that extra sparkle.

• A deep burgundy calla lily works well for the more modern approach to buttonholes (see picture on page 128). I've softened this one by adding in a touch of green hydrangea and angelica root with a single galax leaf.

• Most men are not that keen on wearing a flower on their lapels, so give them something a little more masculine, such as a mixed herb buttonhole (see picture on page 129). I've used a mixture of sage leaves, rosemary sprigs and sedum in this one. Not only does it look great, it also smells divine.

• For the ultra modern, the phalaenopsis orchid buttonhole with lily grass and a strand of wired pearls makes a stunning option (see picture on page 129). This buttonhole with its pearls would be ideal for a groom who wanted to coordinate with his bride's beaded gown.

Every florist's favourite time of year has to be Christmas. I always spend many hours at home decorating the fireplace and tree with pine and cones from the local forest. Christmas allows us to express ourselves in so many ways throughout the home, from table centres to door wreaths – you have endless scope to be creative. In my festive section, I have skimmed through Valentine's Day, Mother's Day, Christmas and White Day. On Valentine's Day in Japan and some other parts of the Far East, women give gifts to men. One month later on White Day, the 14th of March, men return the favour and give gifts to women, typically in the form of a white rose or other white flower. Valentine's Day is one of the busiest times of year in any flower shop. At Jamie Aston, we try to offer something a little different rather than the classic twelve red roses, so in this section I have explained how to make a heart-shaped chocolate box of flowers for those of you who appreciate the quirkier designs.

festive flowers

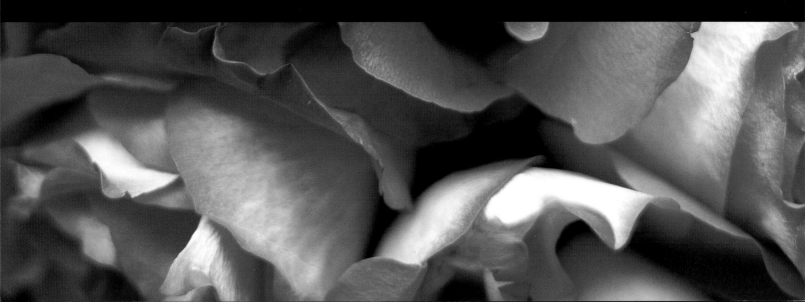

chocolate box

Valentine's Day comes but once a year thankfully! This heart-shaped chocolate box of flowers, although not to everyone's taste, is a quirky little gesture for an unusual gift that will keep you in the hearts of those that receive it.

1 Start by spraying your box with gold spray paint. You need to take your time with this and cover the whole box evenly, including the lid. I find it easier to hold the can approximately 10–13cm away and spray with short bursts of paint. When you spray in one big go, the paint starts to run and form drip marks.

flowers

20 Funky roses

other materials

Heart-shaped box with lid
Gold spray paint
Clear cellophane
1 soaked block of floral foam
Soft pink ribbon

2 Now line your box with a sheet of clear cellophane, which will protect the box from any water leakage and also hold water to help feed the floral foam. Cut off one third of the soaked floral foam. Shave the edges with a knife, so that it's easy to place flower stems into the corners. Place the larger block into the box, then carve the remainder of the floral foam into a triangular piece to fit into the bottom section of the heart-shaped box.

3 Cut most of your rose stems down to approximately 8–10cm long; leave a few stems longer for the top and bottom of the heart. It can be a little tricky to get a heart shape, so you may not get it right first time. Place one rose in the middle of the floral foam, then fill in around this rose, ensuring all the heads remain level with each other.

4 Now add your lid. I have just placed my lid gently on top of the roses to one side. If you want to attach it, tape a wire onto the underside of the lid, then place this through the roses into the floral foam to secure. I have also tied a little piece of ribbon around my lid just to help lift the design.

Variation

You could adapt this design for a friend's birthday by making it less romantic. Use a square or oblong-shaped box and fill with dahlias, hydrangeas, stocks or sweet peas. For a more masculine look, use nutans or green carnations.

white day

Orchids are very popular today; they last for weeks, if not months, and are incredibly easy to maintain. I hate seeing these beautiful phalaenopsis orchids in their plastic pots. This shows how to hide the pots or do away with them completely.

flowers

1 large white phalaenopsis plant

other materials

Tall clear glass vase
Ribbon

1   Take your orchid plant out of its plastic pot and start to pull away at the orchid bark with your hands. Be gentle here, as the roots will just snap off if they are tugged too hard. Once you have most of the orchid bark and dirt off, wash the roots under the tap for a final rinse.

2   Place the washed orchid roots into a clear glass vase filled with water. The orchid should stand up on its own as long as the vase is not too big and the sides of the vase support the orchid. Add a finishing touch by tying a ribbon around the stick that comes with the orchid.

Tips

This method of displaying an orchid plant in water will not kill the plant any faster. I have had phalaenopsis orchids this way in my kitchen for over four months. The trick is to place them in an area which is light, but not bathed in direct sunlight. Don't move them once you are happy with the position. Keep topping up the water regularly to prevent any unsightly chalk marks appearing on the vase.

Variation

For the planted orchid on page 138, I have just placed the orchid in its pot inside a white ceramic cube and then added a few handfuls of flat green moss to secure and disguise the pot.

mother's day

Another busy time of year for florists is Mother's Day, but this time you don't have to go all out and try too hard to impress. Mums in general are happy with the simplest of gestures from their children. Spring flowers are traditionally given on this occasion

and my mother would love me to take her home these planted hyacinth pots. They look fabulous lined up like this on a windowsill or shelf as they all have a different quality about them. But then, I'm sure she would be thrilled for me to take any flowers home.

1   I can't believe I'm even telling you how to do this! Just place each hyacinth into a terracotta pot.

2   Cover the soil with Spanish moss. Pull the moss apart in your hands a little so some of it drapes over the sides of each pot. For a finishing touch, tie a bow around the middle of the pot.

flowers

Fully opened pink hyacinth plants
Spanish moss

other materials

Second-hand mini terracotta pots
Pink ribbon

Tip

Agapanthus, hydrangea and gerbera plants would also make chirpy and colourful pots, as would campanulas which are very delicate and pretty.

Wreaths don't always have to be festive. This autumnal one adds a burst of colour to
any home and can be used as a table centre as well as a door wreath. This wreath is in

wreaths

One of my favourite classes to teach at the school is the winter wreath, which lets us all know the holiday season is upon us! It's such a fun piece to make, allowing for endless creativity. Anyone can make this and it's a great one for the children, too.

autumn wreath

flowers

20 stems of oak foliage

50 orange ranunculus

1 stem of large orange cymbidium orchids

other materials

35cm floral foam wreath frame

1 Soak your floral foam frame in a large bowl of cold water. Shave off a small amount from the inner and outer edges of the frame to create a flatter surface area for your flower stems, helping you to achieve a rounded look. Cut all of your oak to leave approximately 5cm of stem, then simply fill the frame with your oak foliage.

2 Cut your ranunculus and cymbidium down so each flower has a stem of roughly 2.5–5cm in length. Add your orchid heads through the oak in small clusters of three. Finally, add the ranunculus, filling all the gaps with large clusters.

winter wreath

1   Soak your moss in a bowl of water and rinse out as you would a dishcloth. Attach the reel wire onto the wreath frame with a simple knot. Place small hand-sized clumps of moss on top of the wreath frame and bind tightly with the reel wire.

2   Continue to add clumps of moss onto the frame, binding tightly all the way around. Do not cut the wire at the end, as we are now going to bind the pine onto the frame in exactly the same way.

3   Cut all of your pine into 13cm lengths and assemble into little bunches. Place a bunch of pine on top of the moss-covered frame and bind across to secure onto the frame.

4 Place a bunch of a different kind of pine over the bunch you have just bound. It should sit at a slightly different angle so as to cover the binding point of your last bunch. Continue this process until you have covered the whole frame with pine. Alternate your two different types of pine so each type is evenly spread through the design.

5 Wire your cones, birds, crystals and roses (see pages 166–170). Spray each rose head with spray glue and gently dip each head into a pile of iridescent glitter.

6 Attach the roses and pine cones in clusters of three, then attach your doves and crystals evenly through the design. Finally, wire a few strands of crystals or glass beads to the bottom of the wreath frame so they hang elegantly (see picture on page 147).

flowers

1 bag of sphagnum moss

3 bunches of Scotch pine

3 bunches of sugar pine

12 large headed white roses

other materials

Reel wire

35cm wire wreath frame

12 pine cones

9 mini white doves

Strands of crystals or glass beads

Spray glue

Iridescent glitter

festive garland

Christmas is one of the most exciting times of year for any florist. We get to express ourselves through our work at home when decorating the house. I used to love heading off to the woods and rummaging for pine and cones for our fireplace garland. It never looked like this one, mind, but we all start somewhere! This might look daunting and intricate, but it really is just time-consuming. You can cheat and buy ready-made pine garlands which will make it far easier.

flowers

1 bunch of blue pine

20–30 large headed white roses

other materials

2m length of thick string

Reel wire

Spray glue

Iridescent glitter

20 iridescent pine cones

10 decorative butterflies

Strands of pearls or beads

5 artificial frosted branches

1 Make a knot at one end of your string, tying the reel wire onto the string at the same time. Cut your blue pine into 15cm lengths. Hold a few pieces of pine in a bunch and hold over the string. Tightly bind with the reel wire so the pine is attached to the string.

2 Do the same again with another bunch of pine, overlapping your last binding point. Keep going until you reach the end of the string, then simply tie your reel wire into a knot.

Tips

You can just stick the roses into areas of tightly constructed garland to make the whole job quicker and easier, but obviously they will become loose as they dry out.

3 Cut your roses down to 8–10cm. Spray all of them with spray glue and gently dip each rose head into a small pile of iridescent glitter. The glitter will elegantly frame the edge of the rose petals. Using reel wire, attach the roses onto the garland in clusters of three or five. You could place each rose into a water phial if you wanted this display to last a little longer. Alternatively, you could use artificial roses.

4 Wire your pine cones, butterflies and strands of pearls (see page 170). Attach the pine cones to the garland in clusters of three, and disperse the butterflies and pearls evenly through the design.

5 Lastly, add your artificial branches, which you should just push through the pine. You could use any garden twigs here, possibly frosted with fake snow and glitter.

all, you could buy a ten-inch-thick book full of instructions. Now, some of these rules are just common sense; others are informative and worth knowing, and many are just confusing. I have briefly outlined a few of my guidelines in this section. These are the very basics and will see you through this book. Unless you are thinking of going into floristry as a career, you don't need to waste your time on anything else!

tools & techniques

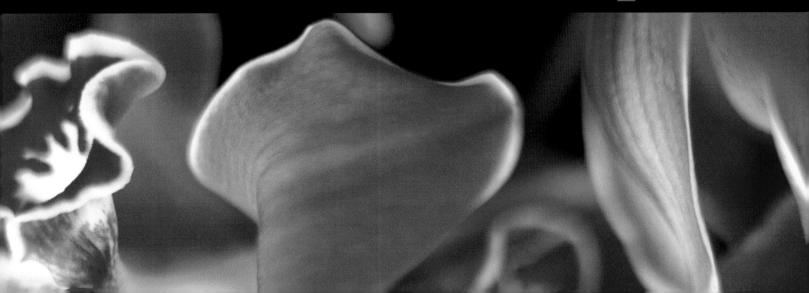

floristry tools

The tools of any trade are fundamental, and this is certainly the case in floristry. Without my floristry scissors, my hands would certainly be a mess! You only need a few basic tools to begin working with flowers: a pair of floristry scissors, a florist's knife, floristry string, pot tape, gutter tape, sharp ribbon scissors and gage wires.

Scissors

I must stress the importance of purchasing a professional pair of floristry scissors from your local garden centre or florist. You will go through many a pair of household scissors if you don't. Floristry scissors are not only sharp but, most importantly, they are designed to protect your hands. The handles on them are made from tough rubber, so they bend with your hands and the pressure you exert.

Knife

Floristry knives are much like any small kitchen knife, but they are not so sharp. They often come with brightly coloured handles to make them harder to lose. This is not an essential product; you can easily make do with a household knife, if you prefer.

String

Floristry string and garden twine is not like regular household string – it breaks more easily when pulled too tight. This makes it ideal for flower bouquets, enabling you to tie your displays securely without damaging them. The string also has a rustic look compared with household nylon string which, in my opinion, does not look as good.

Pot tape

This is used for tying and securing. The beauty of pot tape is its strength and ability to hold under water (ordinary sticky tape would not work in its place). Once the tape has overlapped itself, it becomes even stronger. It is used

to secure floral foam into containers, to secure leaves and flowers in place and to tie delicate bouquets where string might cut into the stems, such as amaryllis and tulips. If you can't get hold of pot tape, I suggest you look for a similar waterproof tape from your local hardware store.

Gutter tape

Gutter tape, or parafilm, is crucial to wiring. Once a stem has been cut for wiring, it will soon dry out. Gutter tape is used to seal the moisture into the stem, therefore increasing its lifespan. Gutter tape also binds all your wires, keeping everything neat and tidy. If you are using metal wires, covering them in gutter tape will prevent them from rusting.

It is best sourced from your local florist but, again, if you are finding it hard to get hold of, you might be able to use a similar product that plumbers use to seal pipes called PTF tape, available from hardware stores.

Wires

Gage wires come in two main forms: bare metal and plastic coated. Their thicknesses and lengths also vary. The thickness of a wire is measured in millimetres with those most commonly used in floristry ranging from 0.24mm to 0.90mm. As wires are used as support tools, it goes hand in hand to say that the heavier the material, the stronger the gage of wire required.

Reel wire comes on a reel rather than pre-cut lengths. It is made of copper and comes in all different colours. It is more expensive than gage wire but is useful for when your wiring needs to be on show, where it can almost be made into a feature. You can buy it in a fine or average thickness, but the average one is the most commonly found and used.

conditioning flowers

Conditioning flowers takes up a large chunk of our mornings at the flower shops. Our flowers arrive from Holland in the same state as when they were picked. The florists have to spend time carefully preparing them for our shop displays and orders.

This can be a time-consuming part of flower arranging, especially on Valentine's Day when you have thousands of red roses to dethorn and condition! Most flowers are easily conditioned – it's just common sense. Ideally, you are looking to remove most of the bottom leaves and any thorns or nasty bits.

CUTTING STEMS

As you know, there are thousands of different types of flowers and foliages out there, and with each different type there comes different care guidelines. Flower stems can be just as amazing as the flowers themselves. Water lilies, for example, have the most fascinating of all stems. When you cut them, you will see lots of little chambers – they look like a kaleidoscope.

The basic rule we all know is always cut stems at an angle. This way, they will have a greater surface area, thus being able to drink more water. This is the case for most stems, but for stems such as amaryllis, I would advise that you cut them straight across, then bind a collar of pot tape around them (see picture opposite). Amaryllis are such heavy flowers and the stems have a tendency to go mushy. When they are cut at an angle, the point of the stem is made weaker, which makes them more prone to buckling under their own weight. By cutting them straight across and taping them to reinforce their strength, you will avoid this.

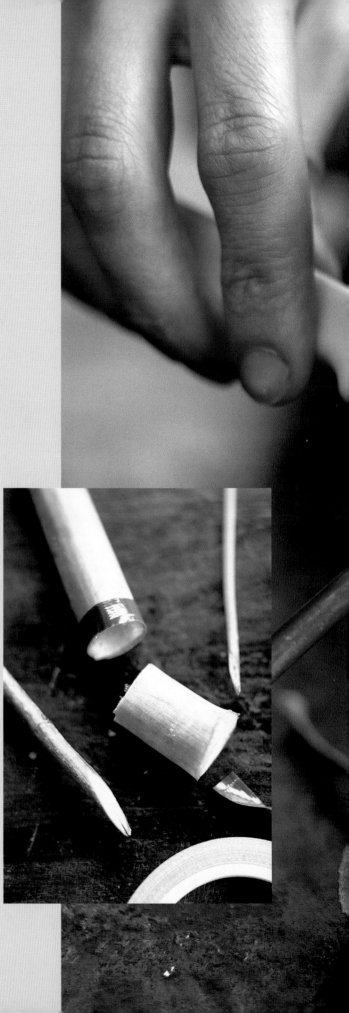

Woody stems

For woody stems such as lilac or hydrangea, I would advise that you first cut them at an angle and then make a small slit up the inside of the stem. This will give them an even bigger surface area. Woody-stemmed flowers are notorious for flopping and drinking badly. You can buy special flower food for woody stems and your florist should supply this when you purchase these kinds of flowers.

Sappy stems

This category mostly covers spring flowers. Flowers such as hyacinths and narcissi are fine if you leave them and don't cut the stems. You will find they take a little longer to bloom, so they last longer. Narcissi, in particular, can release a nasty sap from their cut stems, which can sometimes kill off other flowers.

DETHORNING

A rose stem, for example, will need dethorning and deleafing. Take a floristry knife and gently brush this against the stem of the rose, picking off the lower leaves and all of the thorns.

You need to think ahead when conditioning your flowers and consider what you will be using the flowers for. If you are going to be using long-stemmed roses, for example, and you wanted to use the rose leaves as part of your display, then don't pull them all off! If, however, you are making a compact bridal bouquet where you don't need the leaves, then remove them all at the beginning.

WATER

The idea is to give flowers every chance you can for them to live to their best. Before you start to work with them, it makes sense to prepare them in the best possible way and give them all the help they need to stay fresh. Most flowers need a deep drink before you start to work with them, and it's a good idea to add flower food at all times, which your local florist will provide.

Gerberas

These flowers will often come in a little droopy and are prone to snapping easily. Fill a tall container with water and make a grid of sticky tape over the top. Cut the stems and place the gerberas in so the heads are resting on top of the tape with their stems straight. They will soon assume their upright shape once again, making them easier to work with.

Woody stems

Most flowers will benefit from being left in a deep bucket of water for a short period before you can safely work with them. In particular, flowers with woody stems, such as lilac and hydrangea, and foliage drink more slowly, because they're harder and not so open. Don't neglect your foliage; it needs to drink as much as your flowers!

Porous stems

Calla lilies, arum lilies and amaryllis have quite porous stems, which means they can turn to mush fairly quickly. Add just enough water to cover the bottom of the stems to prevent this from happening.

Changing water

Water should be changed and stems re-cut every three days on average, with new flower food added each time. This helps to keep bacteria at bay. Bacteria forms in the water and around cut stems very quickly, so in doing this you're prolonging the life of the flowers. Caring for your vase arrangements in this way will keep them looking and smelling fresh.

GETTING RID OF POLLEN

We have all experienced pollen on our clothes. It's awful stuff and once you've rubbed it in, it's very difficult to get out. Always remove pollen stamens at the first opportunity. You will find that by catching them early, they will not be so far developed and messy. Some people cut them out; I prefer just to pull them out – I don't like the look you get when you have neatly cut stamens at the heart of a flower. By pulling on them, the stamens remain intact but the pollen is removed.

It's not only a good idea to remove the pollen because of the danger of it coming into contact with your clothes, but also for the aesthetics of the flower. When pollen starts to drop, it can end up ruining the look of a flower, especially on amaryllis stems. They have such delicate petals and last for such a long time, so it's a shame to see the most perfect of petals covered in pollen because you forgot to remove it.

Jamie's top ten tips

1 If your fresh hydrangea wilts straightaway, cut the stems and place the whole hydrangea stem up to the neck of the flower into a deep bucket of water. Leave this for a few hours and, nine times out of ten, the hydrangea will revive itself.

2 Spray hydrangea petals with water; you will find they live longer this way.

3 If you get pollen on your clothes, use a piece of foam (much like what is used in chairs and upholstery) to dab on the pollen. The foam acts like a magnet and lifts it right off. Sticky tape can often do more damage as it presses pollen into the fabric. Ask your florist for this type of foam or buy from a fabric shop.

4 Stick a pin in a tulip just below the head and you'll find the stem will grow straight instead of flopping over.

5 Tulips and hyacinths continue to grow once they have been picked or cut.

6 Many florists wire gerberas to strengthen them, but I prefer not to do this because it doesn't look natural. If they are prepared as explained on page 162, you won't have a problem.

7 To make your own flower food, add a couple of drops of household bleach and a few teaspoons of sugar to a cup of warm water. Stir well until dissolved and add to your vase of water.

8 If your flowers are too closed and you need them to be more open for an arrangement, simply place them in a container of warm water, add flower food and position under strong light, ideally natural light.

9 Anthuriums are delivered to florists in plastic water phials, so it's worth asking your local florist if they have any they can spare.

10 When working with soft-stemmed flowers, either make a small hole in the floral foam using a pen or pencil for a guide hole, or insert a wire through the stem upwards (see page 166) to strengthen it before you work it into the floral foam.

soaking floral foam

Floral foam comes in many forms, the most common of which is Oasis. The foam acts much like a sponge, soaking up and retaining water. Once soaked, the floral foam is as an ideal base for arranging flowers.

Floral foam is widely available and comes in many different shapes and sizes – the most common of these being small blocks the size of a house brick. To soak the foam, you need to fill a large container with cold water – if you want, you can add flower food to this. Place your block of floral foam on top of the water and let the foam sink by itself. It will take a few minutes for it to soak up the water evenly, so it's important you remain patient and refrain from pushing the block down under the water. Pushing the foam down will only result in large gaps of dry foam on the inside, and placing flowers into one of them will result in a dead flower display before you know it.

1 As you can see, I have just placed this block of floral foam on top of the water.

2 The foam has completely sunk by itself and is floating just under the water line. It's now ready to use.

wiring

We wire flower heads when we need to create neat, compact displays, or when we want to manipulate flower heads into an unnatural form. Wiring is most commonly used for buttonholes, headdresses and bridal bouquets. Most of our students find wiring therapeutic and calming, and once you get the hang of it, it's fairly easy.

When you wire a flower head, you are really just replacing the stem with a thin metal wire. The flower head, once wired, is sealed with gutter tape, which helps keep the moisture in and prevents the flowers from drying out too quickly.

Flowers obviously don't last as long when wired; a wired rose buttonhole, for example, will last for about two days in the fridge. Once out of the fridge and worn, it will last for about eight hours.

Roses are one of most popular flowers for wiring and last fairly well. Carnations, along with tropical, waxy flowers, such as cymbidium orchids, anthuriums and calla lilies, are also popular and last longer, because they're used to surviving on little water. More delicate flowers, such as peonies and dahlias, don't last so long, but again can be kept in the fridge (as long as it's no colder than 8°C) or other cool place until needed.

My opinion is that you don't always need the wires specified – it's not going to ruin your display if you can't lay your hands on a 0.44mm wire, for instance. Provided the wire you have holds the flower securely, don't worry too much about sourcing specific gages.

WIRING A ROSE

This technique can be used for any other flowers with a large single head similar to a rose, such as ranunculus, arum lilies, dahlias, gerberas and carnations.

1   Cut the rose head from its stem, leaving approximately 2.5cm of stem. Take a 0.56mm gage wire and place this up inside the stem of the rose until it feels secure.

Note

Gutter tape needs to be stretched and manipulated around the stems and wires. You need to have your fingers close together, keeping the gutter tape taut at all times. If your hands are wet or even a bit sweaty, this will be very hard to do. Gutter tape is notorious for unravelling on itself. The best way to master this skill is to just keep guttering the same stem until you are confident.

2 Thread a 0.44mm gage wire through the stem of the rose.

3 Bring the 0.44mm wire down to meet the 0.56mm wire and twist one half of this wire around the other roughly three times.

4 Cut your wires to the length you need, then gutter-tape them right to the end.

WIRING A LEAF

More delicate flowers or those that are made up of lots of little flower heads can also be wired in this way – take, for example, the lilacs and bouvardia in the headdress project on page 120. Rather than stitch the flower itself as shown here in step 1, just thread the wire between the little flower heads, bring it back down and continue as per step 3.

1   Cut the leaf from its stem, so there is approximately 2.5cm of stem left. Thread a 0.28mm gage wire through the middle, much like making a small stitch in the leaf.

2   Bring each end of the wire down to meet the stem and twist a couple of times. Now place a 0.44mm gage wire behind the stem of the leaf (this wire will provide support and length).

3   Bring the 0.44mm gage wire down and around the stem and bind one leg of the wire around all the others a couple of times.

4   Cut your wires to the length you need, then gutter-tape them right to the end.

WIRING PROPS

Wires aren't just used on flowers and foliage; they are also widely used by florists to wire products, such as fruit, berries, cones, cinnamon sticks and fabric.

Throughout this book, I have used several different types of product other than flowers in my work. This photograph shows how I've attached these different items onto wires, so that I can work them through my designs.

In this case, I have pierced the little bird with a heavy wire, wrapped a thick wire around the pearls, and wired the bunch of feathers in the same way as a rose head. Basically, you don't need to worry about any rules here, just use your common sense and wire the chosen object in the neatest and easiest possible way you can see. It really is not that difficult.

When it comes to wiring fruit, say an apple, the best way is to place two thick wires straight through the apple on either side so you end up with a cross, then bring the wires down to meet each other.

To wire fabric, poke the wire though the centre of the fabric, then bring both ends of the wire together and twist two or three times to secure.

You do not need to gutter-tape your wires when they are securing props. The only time you might need to do this is if you wanted to seal or cover the metal wires to prevent them from rusting. This can be a good idea if the display is being used on delicate surfaces, or if you had wired some lace through a bridal bouquet – this avoids rust marks!

Index

acknowledgements

What a year! I'm not quite sure where it's gone but what we have achieved in this book makes me extremely proud and I am eternally grateful to so many people.

I have met and worked with the best team I could have imagined on this book. Firstly, thank you to Muna for suggesting the project. Thank you so much Jenny for all of your encouragement and calming influence, you're a true credit to the team at Kyle Cathie. Darling Nicky, thank you for all the laughs and for an amazing design job, you really have pulled out all the stops to get this book to print. Ditte, what a photographer! I love your work – from day one your portfolio stood out above all the rest. We are all privileged to have worked with you on this project, and your energy is truly inspirational. Thank you Vanessa for your superb editorial input and Tabitha for your inspired selection of props.

Thank you to all the locations we shot at, including Georgia at Brondesbury Road, Rose at the Old Dairy and of course Diana Henry for your beautiful house and amazing lunches. Thank you to Bobbie, Dannie, Tina, Michelle and Jenny for modelling. Many thanks to Laura Ashley and Jenny Packham for the generous contributions of props and dresses for our photoshoots.

Heartfelt thanks to all of my colleagues at Jamie Aston, in particular Ji-Young, Irena, Andrea, Jackie, John, Terry and Gary and most importantly the amazing Jan Goodhill for all of your encouragement and support.

Finally, thank you to my much loved and adored family; Mum, Dad, Lisa and Henry.

Marnix, thank you for really supporting me and being so understanding, you keep me going. x